DID YOU KNOW? Monkeys

DID YOU KNOW?

Monkeys

young reed

Contents

What is a Monkey?

- Monkeys are a large family of **mammals** with more than **three hundred species** in existence around the world.

- They vary in size from the **one-metre-long Mandrill** from Africa to the **fifteen-centimetre-long Pygmy Marmoset** from South America. A large male Mandrill can weigh up to thirty-seven kilograms, which is about **three hundred times heavier** than the average marmoset.

- Monkeys are **primates**, meaning that they are related to humans. They share certain features with us, like a relatively **large brain** and many have **thumbs** on their hands to help grasp food or tree branches.

Mandrill

Pygmy Marmoset

- They have a **tail**, which can be very long in some species such as spider monkeys and very short in others such as baboons.

What's NOT a Monkey?

● **Apes** belong on a slightly different branch of the primate family tree compared to monkeys. Members of the ape family have **no tail**, a **broader chest**, and are more likely to **walk on two legs** than a monkey.

Gibbon.

Chimpanzees.

- **Chimpanzees, Bonobos, Gorillas, Orang-utans** and **Gibbons** are all apes, as of course are **Humans**.
- Other primates that look a bit like monkeys, but belong in different families, include **Lemurs** and **Tarsiers**.

Ring-tailed Lemur.

Tarsier.

Fascinating facts

- Monkeys are often very social animals that live in families or larger groups. They often work together to search for food and spend time grooming each other.
- Many monkeys have opposable thumbs – like humans – to help them grasp on to food and branches.

You can see similarities between a monkey's hands and feet and our own.

Groups of monkeys love to groom each other.

● A group of monkeys is known as a troop.

Special adaptations

- Monkeys' **long tails** help them to balance while running or jumping.
- Some species have a **prehensile tail**, which can grab onto tree branches and act like an extra arm.

- Monkeys rely strongly on their **eyesight** for finding food compared to other primates such as lemurs, which use their sense of smell. Some monkeys, including Night Monkeys, are **nocturnal** and have huge eyes to help them see in the dark.

Spider Monkey using its prehensile tail.

Night Monkeys are sometimes known as 'owl monkeys' because of their big owl-like eyes.

Where do they live?

- Different species of monkeys are found around the world – they are found in many parts of **Africa, Asia** and **Central** and **South America**.

Black-and-white Colobus Monkeys in an African forest.

- The greatest numbers of different species can be found in warm and wet environments such as **jungles** and **rainforests**.

- Some monkeys are found in open rocky **habitats** with few trees, such as the **Gelada** in the mountains of Ethiopia.

● Japanese Macaques are able to live in freezing snowy conditions during winter. Famously, they help to keep themselves warm by bathing in hot water from springs.

Gelada.

Japanese Macaque.

Territory matters

- Monkeys will **mark their territory** with wee and other scents from their body to keep rivals off their patch.

This facial expression says 'keep away!'

- As well as sound, monkeys use **facial expressions** and other **body movements** to communicate between members of a family or troop.

- If all else fails, a dispute may end up in a fight.

● Some monkeys communicate and defend their territories using sound. Howler Monkeys are among the loudest – their calls sound like thunder rumbling through the South American rainforest. The calls carry for up to five kilometres.

Howler Monkey howling.

What's for dinner?

- **Fruits, seeds, nuts, leaves** and other parts of plants make up the bulk of the diet of many monkeys.

- They will also eat **small animals** such as lizards and insects.

- Because monkeys eat both plants and animals we describe them as **omnivores.**

- And, of course, when monkeys come into contact with humans there is always the chance of a **free handout.**

Family life

- Most monkey mums give birth to **one baby** at a time, although some of the smaller species such as tamarins and marmosets often have **twins**.
- The baby relies on its **mother's milk** for the first few months of life.
- In many species the **baby's relatives** – brothers, sisters, cousins and aunts – will help to bring up the youngster. There's no shortage of **babysitters**!
- A young monkey becomes an **adult after two years** for bigger species, or one year for smaller ones.

Baby monkeys often hitch a lift on mum's back.

Young babies rely on milk from their mother.

Monkeys and people

- Some monkey species **thrive in human towns and cities** – for example macaques are common in many Asian cities.
- Other species with specialised requirements have become rare and endangered because of **human activities** leading to **deforestation** and the loss of the habitat they rely upon for food and shelter.

Macaques are a familiar sight around many temples in Asia.